THE
MUDPIES
BOOK OF
BOREDOM
BUSTERS

THE MUDPIES BOOK OF BOREDOM BUSTERS

by Nancy Blakey

Illustrations by Alexandra Foley

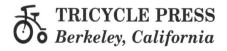
TRICYCLE PRESS
Berkeley, California

TRICYCLE PRESS
P.O. Box 7123
Berkeley, California 94707
www.tenspeed.com

Typeset in New Century Schoolbook

Library of Congress Cataloging-in-Publication Data

Blakey, Nancy.
    The mudpies book of boredom busters / by Nancy Blakey.
        p. cm.
    Includes index.
    ISBN 1-883672-86-4 (alk. paper)
    1. Creative activities and seat work. I. Title.
    LB1537.B617   1999
    372.5--dc21   99-17791
                                    CIP

First printing, 1999
Printed in Canada

1 2 3 4 5 6 — 03 02 01 00 99

For all parents and kids who are unafraid of boredom,
and the places it can take you

Contents

Boredom: *Prescription for Adventure*

Our lives begin with family. If there is optimism, children grow into their adult selves hopeful, radiant with possibilities, and holding on to a clutch of memories that helped to shape their lens of the world. The good memories, the bad. The hurts and yowls. Splendid summer nights. The kisses at the right moment. Reprimands at the wrong. A world shaped invisibly by color and feelings, smells and textures. These memories place us where we are, define who we want to be.

The memories our children take with them are not the clean house, the board meetings, or the number of clients added to our list. It is the yeses they remember. The night tag and snowmen, cupcakes, mud, and flower seeds. The yeses at the kitchen table, in the backyard, on a bed at night telling stories. The little time left in our busy days urges us to say no. Tomorrow. We are tired. Waiting for the good day to make a memory that never arrives.

As I write this for a fast approaching deadline, my son enters the room. Nick is bored. He asks to make a cake and a luscious but lengthy frosting that requires my help (see page 79 for the recipe). All I can think of is the entirely possible mess, the short hours left to me. "NO!" I want to scream crazily. "I am writing something important!" I close my eyes and laugh at his timing. I say yes. The cake is baked. The dishes are washed with spilling boy-energy. The words will turn up on time.

The day has arrived. It is right now, while deadlines are being met, laundry folded, and another workday draws to a close. Sometimes it takes a child's boredom to bring us there.

I remember being bored as a child. In the summer, after chores, my mother pushed my brothers and sisters and me out the back door and into a dull landscape of wheat fields and irrigation ditches. "Find something to do!" she ordered.

The first tentative nudge of boredom is a ticklish thing. It itches, but you don't know where or what to scratch. It makes you sigh and snort. You are testy and a little fearful. It feels dangerous. Forever. As if boredom will dog you past all adventure and fun and the day will end empty and meaningless.

We had no choice. We were driven to catch frogs and build forts. We made lemonade stands and played baseball with invented rules and moving bases. Over the years I moved reluctantly through boredom's idle territory. I would be a different person without the paths it delivered. For boredom often pressed me to read extraordinary books, to take walks, and to meet new people. Boredom volunteered me, sent me to foreign countries, and pushed me out of dead-end jobs. Boredom led me to believe the only forward is through.

I have watched our four children wrestle with their own bouts of boredom, their energy a friction that smelled like burning rubber. When they were young, they wheedled and begged for television, video games, Nintendo. Have your own adventures! I told them. Whittle sticks, catch frogs, build a fort, wash the dog! I did when I was your age!

Of course they refused. I expected them to. It sounded utterly tedious, like a long list of sweaty chores from Old Mother Hubbard.

Looked at another way, boredom is an invitation to our own party of events. Not an instructor's or a parent's. Not guided or managed or improved by a mother's tiresome list. It is a personal itch that needs to be scratched.

When we accept the invitation, something magical happens. Passions are born. Interests are developed. An inner fund of resources develops. The same resources we use for a meaningful life. Without this fund, boredom can push our children to self-destruction: drugs, violence, and random pranks that eat up their young lives and spit them out. We are left to pick up the pieces and wonder what went wrong.

In an attempt to save our children, we sign them up for sports, classes, camps, and workshops. We let them watch too much television, play on the computer. We keep them busy, their hours filled with our chore list of activities. They learn, too young, to live like we do: overly full days, not enough time.

I believe it is important to allow children a taste of boredom while they are young and under your watchful eye. To measure it into their bones and muscles like a rare fuel to propel them forward. It is important to preempt a child's time from television, from organized activities, and spend it instead on claiming her imagination. For in the end, that is all we have. If a thing cannot be imagined first—

a cake, a relationship, a cure for AIDS—it cannot *be*. Our lives are bound by what we can envision. If we have no experience with the process of imagination, how can we imagine the possibilities ahead?

I cannot plant that imagination into my children. I *can* provide the environment where their creativity is not just another mess to clean up, but is welcome evidence of grappling successfully with boredom.

It is possible for boredom to deliver us to our best selves. The self that longs for risk and illumination and unspeakable beauty. If we sit still long enough, we may hear the call behind boredom. With practice, we may have the imagination to rise up from the emptiness and answer it.

The Mudpies Boredom Busters Book is a book of ideas for the days you allow your child a little boredom. It can be difficult to draw a child's interest into a creative project. (I have even used the Brer Rabbit approach, and started one myself—"Please don't do this project with me. It is mine! I want to do it myself! You probably won't like it anyway." This can seriously prick some interest.) Tell your child you understand she is bored and that you have a few ideas for her. If she refuses your offering, place this book in front of her and leave the room. Don't give in! She is in the middle of the rich and wondrous process of learning what to do when there is nothing to do. In the end, it is up to your child to decide if she will run with it. The environment where the ideas take hold and the projects take place is up to you. Give your child the time and space to move through boredom. The rewards are an investment in a meaningful future.

Out of Doors

PVC Pipe Structures

The best kind of projects are those without a "right" and "wrong" way of doing things. When a child is allowed to manipulate materials according to an inner recipe, the results will build confidence, boost creativity, and increase problem-solving skills.

PVC pipe and fittings are an inexpensive medium for kids to create on a grand scale outdoors. Provide a variety of pipe lengths and fittings to join the pieces, and your child can create anything from ladders and forts to free form sculptures.

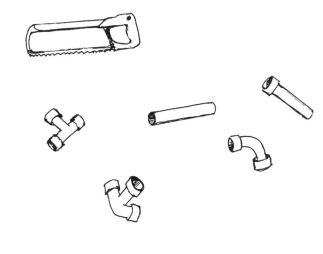

What you will need:

PVC pipe (1- or 2-inch is a good size. Be sure to buy enough! Start with at least 50 feet.)

hacksaw

pipe fittings including four-way, three-way, T, and angled

Saw the pipe into desired lengths with the hacksaw. Place the fittings in a box and have your child place the pipe pieces into the fittings. She will soon learn to select the right angle and number of fittings to reproduce the idea in her head. Take a photo of the creation!

Camp Craft

Nothing beats sleeping outdoors on a warm summer night. Whether it is in your backyard or in the wilderness, try out one or two of the following projects. After you demonstrate the safety rules of sawing and whittling, your child will be grateful if you put the steps to these projects in his hands. When parents intervene to make things more efficient, we immediately distance our children from the process. Your job is to join your child in the evening, and talk about the wondrous tent he made, the clever fork, and to point out the Perseid meteor shower that appears in the August night sky.

Tarp Tent

Tarps, along with duct tape, are versatile tools to have on hand. This tent can serve as a fort during the day and a shelter at night.

What you will need:

rope or clothesline

2 trees

small tarp (available at hardware stores)

stakes (metal tent stakes work best, but you can also use wooden stakes)

twine

String the rope or clothesline between two trees at shoulder height. Place the tarp over the rope, and pull the edges out until they meet the ground evenly. Adjust the height of the rope if necessary. If you are using tent stakes, space them evenly in the tarp grommets, and hammer them into the ground. For wooden stakes, hammer them in beside the tarp edge, then thread the twine through the tarp grommet and tie it to the stake.

Handy Hook

There is a pioneer spirit to camping that appeals to kids of all ages. This hand-made hook has been around for centuries and serves a useful function even today.

What you will need:

thin rope or twine

V-shaped small branch

small handsaw

Use the rope to secure one side of the V-shaped branch to a tree, leaving the other side to poke out and form a hook. Hitches and half hitches work well to secure the hook to the tree. (Show your child how to tie these essential knots, then let her attempt them!) You may have to use the handsaw to trim the main stem leading to the V to get the hook to hang properly. Hang a backpack or a portable shower from your hook. Solar-powered portable showers are available at sporting good stores and make an excellent addition to outdoor activities.

Wooden Cooking Tools

This activity is for older children who are capable of using a pocketknife with adult supervision. Many parents who allow their children to watch horrific violence on television are reluctant to give their children a pocketknife—perhaps with good reason! I have found over the years that when responsible children are given a task using an adult tool with supervision, they reliably live up to our trust and are honored. The trick is to have a purpose for the pocketknife. Here are three.

Marshmallow Stick

We all remember making these at one time or another! Find a long skinny branch. (This is a good time to talk to your child about ecological considerations: two ideas you can discuss are not destroying a live plant for your temporary needs, and leaving the environment as if you have never been there.) Whittle one end of the stick to a point. Place your marshmallow on the pointed end, and toast it over the coals of a fire or barbecue grill.

Cooking Whip

Find a thin branch with three smaller twigs that have grown from the main stem. Cut it to a cooking utensil length. Whittle the three twigs to points. Use it to whip your eggs or stir the pancake batter.

Fork

Need a big fork to turn your meat? Find a thin branch that forks into a V-shape. Cut the tines down to the desired length and whittle the end of each tine to a point. Make two forks and use them as salad utensils.

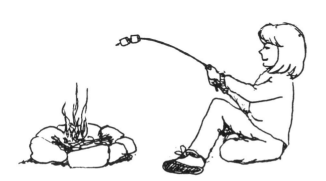

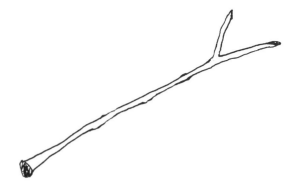

Making the World More Beautiful

One of our all-time favorite books is *Miss Rumphius* by Barbara Cooney, a luminous book about contributing to the world. After much thought and many adventures, Miss Rumphius decides to scatter lupine seeds along the roadsides. It becomes a simple gift of glorious color each spring and lives on long past Miss Rumphius. Your family can offer the same gift to your community by scattering wildflower seeds along the roads that lead to your home. Be sure to scatter only seeds native to your area. We save foxglove seeds every autumn from our garden and spread them in the spring along the margins of our neighborhood. Your child will be reminded of his contribution as the flowers burst into color over the summer.

Spend an afternoon picking up litter with your child. Wear rubber gloves and bring along two heavy-duty garbage bags. Use one for garbage and one for recyclable goods like aluminum cans and bottles. You may be surprised at the items found along the roads. One year we discovered a perfectly good hammer and a Barbie doll!

The Mudpies Book of Boredom Busters

Start a compost pile. It can be as simple as a small pile in the corner of your yard. Begin with a layer of dirt mixed with yard waste. Save fruit and vegetable peelings in a small plastic bucket under the sink. Empty the bucket of waste into the dirt mixture and mix together with a shovel. Add worms (available at many nurseries or perhaps from a friend who has a compost pile). Add another layer of dirt to cap the new mix. Before adding new organic waste, dig and turn the compost. Water if it gets dry. In a short time, and with surprisingly little fuss, you will have a pile of rich, dark soil to add to your garden. In the end, you will be doubly blessed with your compost project: plants will grow healthy and vigorous with the addition of compost, and you will reduce the amount of garbage your household generates.

Pillow Pak Planting

This is a type of container gardening that requires little space and reliably produces great results! Make sure you place your pillow where there is plenty of sun.

What you will need:

3 cubic feet of potting soil (3 large bags)

large plastic bucket or bin to mix soil

large industrial-strength garbage bag

stapler

plants: tomato, lettuce, flowers, or herbs

Pour the bags of potting soil into the large bucket. Stir in enough water to moisten the mixture, but not make mud. Place the damp soil in the garbage bag, fold the end down, and staple it shut. Place the pillow on its side in a sunny spot, pushing the soil around inside until it is distributed evenly. Using a sharp knife, make an X where you will be planting your vegetables. Space the plants so there is plenty of room between them to grow. For example, lettuce plants should be spaced approximately a foot apart. The pillow can accommodate one large tomato plant. Place the plant in the cut-out X, and cover the roots. Water your pillow pak sparingly (once every 10 days to 2 weeks). Because there is no drainage, it is easy to drown the plants and cause root rot.

The black plastic will absorb the sun and accelerate the growth of your plants. After a few months, the nutrients from the potting soil will be used up and you will need to fertilize your plants with a good liquid fertilizer diluted in water.

Seed Markers

Mark your garden with distinction! At the end of the season, save the tags for next year.

What you will need:

disposable aluminum cookie tray

newspapers

blunt pencil

hot glue gun

bamboo skewers

Cut a small piece from the aluminum tray. Lay newspapers down for a pad, then using the blunt pencil, engrave a picture of the plant and/or the name on the aluminum piece. Use your imagination! Scallop the edges with scissors, or add decorations to the marker. Next, with adult supervision, glue or tape the marker to a skewer and plant in the garden at the head of the seed row.

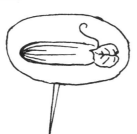

Taters in a Tire

Potatoes were the first thing we ever planted. My then-three-year-old son took a few from our cupboard and, unbeknownst to me, simply stuck them in the ground. We were all amazed with a bumper crop of potatoes in the fall! Potatoes are one of the easiest and most satisfying plants for kids to grow. Not much garden space? Plant them in recycled tires!

What you will need:

compost or steer manure

good soil

6 recycled tires

3 or 4 seed potatoes

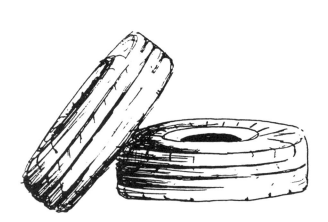

The Mudpies Book of Boredom Busters

Find a sunny, level place in the garden. Mix equal amounts of compost (or steer manure) with your garden soil. Stack two tires on top of each other and place the soil mixture into the tires. Examine the potatoes. Each one has several eyes that will sprout. Cut the potatoes into chunks, with each piece having an eye. Space the potato pieces in the tires, cover with more soil, and water the soil until damp. Keep in mind, water is important for potatoes to grow nice and fat. When the weather is dry, remember to water them!

When the potato plant is established, add another tire and more soil to the stack, leaving some foliage above the dirt. Over the summer, as your plant grows, continue to add tires and soil. Potatoes will grow along the soil-covered stem as you add the tires. In the fall, when the plant looks dead, the potatoes are ready to harvest—the best part! Remove the tires and reap the bounty!

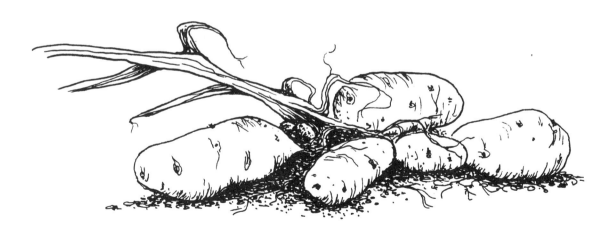

Worm Bin

We've had a compost pile in the corner of our yard for years. We don't consider ourselves zealous gardeners or farmers, but we do love our compost for many reasons: for the brilliant colors it coaxes from our flowers, for the fat and juicy carrots it helps produce, for making the lavender smell deeper, but most of all we love the compost pile for the worms—lots of worms, hundreds and thousands of worms! The kids fish with them and feed them to their lizards. They sell them, save starving baby birds with them, and use them in science fair projects. We like worms.

For people who do not have the space for a compost pile, worm bins are a wonderful alternative. They reduce household garbage, produce what gardeners call brown gold (worm poop in kids' terms) for the vegetable patch or planter box, and provide one of the most fascinating ongoing projects you will ever do with your kids. Rest assured that worms are quiet, clean, and polite guests. They eat fruit and vegetable scraps, leftover cereal, and crushed egg shells. Worms adore coffee grounds and tea leaves (paper filters and bags included). About the only things you should avoid placing in your bin are animal or dairy products. With a small investment of time and energy, you can reap the rewards of healthier plants and the satisfaction of helping our environment.

What you will need:

stack of old newspapers

large plastic storage bin with lid (available at your hardware store)

hammer and big nails, or drill with big bit

1 pound red worms (Eisenia foetida) (available at many plant nurseries or fishing supply stores)

The Mudpies Book of Boredom Busters

To prepare the bin for the worms, hammer or drill several rows of drainage holes at the bottom of the storage bin. Good air circulation is also important, so hammer or drill a row of breathing holes along the top edge of the bin and several rows in the lid.

To make the bedding, shred or cut a pile of newspapers into thin strips. Don't worry about newspaper ink; toxic heavy metals are no longer used. Soak the strips in a bucket or sink of water, then squeeze the paper until you barely have a drop of water dripping from the paper. (The paper should be damp, not dripping.) Fluff up the damp shreds of paper and place them in the bin. Continue wetting and squeezing the strips of paper until you have several inches of bedding. At this point you can add dried leaves, a little damp peat moss, or dirt from your compost.

Add the worms. You cannot use earthworms because they need a mineral soil and do not compost organic waste the way red worms do. Feed your worms around 3 pounds of food waste a week. We don't measure, we simply bury our leftover oatmeal, pasta, apple cores, carrot peelings, or whatever vegetable or fruit food waste we have. Bury the waste in different parts of the bin to distribute the food evenly. Replace the lid and keep the bin in a place where it does not get under 55 degrees or over 75 degrees (underneath a kitchen sink, or in the garage in summer).

After several months, you should have a rich form of dirt called vermicompost. Mix it with peat moss and vermiculite for a lush potting soil.

Seed Starter

Want to involve your child in gardening? Let him grow his own plants! Radish and sunflower seeds are exceptionally gratifying because they sprout quickly and are easy to grow.

What you will need:

potting soil

old pan or bowl

egg carton

seeds (radish or sunflower)

Place a quart or two of potting soil in the pan or bowl. Stir in enough water (or use your hands) to dampen the soil, but not make mud. Place the soil into the cups of the egg carton, and push a seed into the center of each cup. Cover loosely with more soil. Place the seed starter in a sunny place in your home. Water when the soil is dry to the touch, but not too much! Transplant outdoors in the garden when the sprouts have more than two leaves each.

String Game in the Woods

You don't need the woods to do this activity— a backyard will do.

What you will need:

1 ball of string, yarn, or twine per player

small prize per player (a certificate for a favor, a small toy, a flashlight for night tag, etc.)

paper and felt-tip marker to make a name tag for each player

Begin by tying a prize to one end of the string. Place the prize in a hiding place in the woods and then unroll the ball of string as you walk around bushes, cross streams, wind through trees, and zig-zag your way to the starting place you have chosen. It can be a long journey for older children, shorter and easier for younger. Tie name tag to the end. Repeat the process for each player.

When you are ready to start, remind the children to roll up the string as they go along and recycle it for another use.

Outdoor Science for Summer Days

Is there a better place than a wading pool on a hot summer day for science activities? The following projects are wonderful alternatives to the there-isn't-anything-to-do blues. It is hard to be bored racing boats while learning the principles of physics and chemical reactions! All you need are a wading pool or a body of water and a few simple ingredients. Be sure to supervise all young children closely while they are near water.

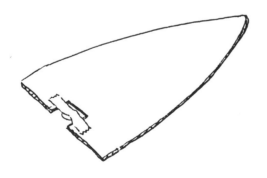

Soap Boat

This boat moves like magic. Try it before your child gets in the water, and again while he is in the pool.

What you will need:

piece of thin cardboard (like the side of a cereal box)

sliver of soap

tape

Cut the cardboard into the shape of a boat with a pointed bow. Notch the stern of the boat to make a space for the soap. Next, secure the small piece of soap in the notch with the tape. Place your boat in the pool.

What happens? The soap breaks the surface tension of the water, propelling the boat. The stronger surface tension in front of the boat pulls it forward.

CO₂ Boat

This boat is wondrously propelled by the chemical reaction of baking soda mixed with vinegar.

What you will need:

corkscrew

small empty plastic soda pop bottle with cap

straw that bends

small scissors

small piece of clay

vinegar

baking soda

tissue

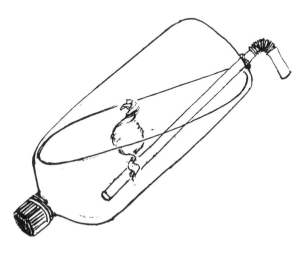

Use the corkscrew to make a small hole in the bottom of the bottle near an edge. Make the hole just big enough to fit the straw through (you may have to use a small pair of scissors to cut away the plastic). Push the straw through the hole, leaving the bending part of the straw outside the bottle. Seal the hole around the straw with the clay.

Are you ready? Remove the cap from the bottle and pour in about ⅓ cup vinegar (exact proportions are not necessary). Pour a tablespoon of baking soda onto a small piece of tissue, wrap it up, and twist the ends tightly. Slip the tissue packet into the vinegar, replace the cap, and set the bottle-boat on the water with the straw bent down into the water.

What happens? The baking soda (a base) reacts with the vinegar (an acid) to create carbon dioxide. The boat is propelled around the pool by the released carbon dioxide through the straw.

Magic Fingers

This activity can be done over and over again. It looks like magic!

What you will need:

small plastic soda pop bottle

corkscrew

Make a small hole near the bottom of the plastic bottle with the corkscrew or a knife. Fill the bottle with water and watch it spring from the hole you just made. Now cover the top of the bottle with your hand.

What happens? The water magically stops flowing. When air cannot move in to replace the water draining from the bottle, it effectively stops the movement of the water. As soon as you remove your hand, the water flows out because air is allowed into the space vacated by the water.

Obstacle Course

Obstacle courses, by their very nature, invite a child's mind and body to work together, and this is a great activity to unleash that focused energy!

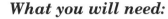

What you will need:

various items to create stations: a large cardboard box, ladder, old tires (available free at most tire stores), a jump rope, chairs, a box of old clothes, an old mattress, hula hoops, balls, sticks for a slalom course, a wheelbarrow, chalk, a bucket, a piece of rope, a marble, a coffee can, 2-by-6 boards (any length), a broomstick

stopwatch

For a successful obstacle course, create stations that are age appropriate. Here are several ideas for stations, but feel free to adapt and add your own. Organize the stations throughout the yard. It helps to number them so it is clear which order to do them in. You can time the obstacle course with the stopwatch if you like.

Here are the stations in no particular order:

- Place a broomstick between two chairs to create a jump.
- Remove your shoes, pick up a marble with your toes, and place it in a coffee can.
- Pile old tires up for a climb, or lay out 2 wide and 3 long to run through (one foot in each tire on either side).
- Crawl through a large box opened at both ends.
- Lay a ladder on the ground and, holding one foot, hop through the rungs.
- Jump rope 10 times without missing.
- Somersault down an old mattress or sleeping bag pad.
- Lay 8 sticks in a zig-zag pattern and run, slalom-like, through them.
- Run around a tree or shrub 3 times.
- Crawl under a row of chairs.
- Rest yourself on your feet and hands, lift, and make a table with your tummy. Place a tennis ball on your tummy and crawl like this without dropping the ball.
- Put on some old dress-up clothes over your own clothes and race to the next station where you will take them off.
- Hula hoop 8 times.
- Set several hula hoops within hopping distance of each other. Hop from inside one hoop to the next.
- Climb a tree (if available).
- Run down 2-by-6 boards laid end to end without allowing your feet to touch the ground.

The Mudpies Book of Boredom Busters

Night Tag

A game of tag on a summer night is thrilling. Listening to the calls and laughter may bring back memories of your own childhood. The dishes can wait. Join the game!

What you will need:

*laundry basket with a
ball, beanbag, or other
small object in it*

*flashlight for the person
who is "It"*

The object of the game is for the players to retrieve the ball from the laundry basket. The person who is It can freeze the players with one bolt of light from the flashlight. The person who is frozen can be freed by the touch of another player. Your children can make up other rules as they go along (which is a sign of a healthy game!).

Water Slide

The commercial Slip-n-Slide has been discontinued for a good reason: it can be dangerous if the slide is placed on a slope near stationary objects such as trees or fences. I am including a homemade version of the water slide because, with safety rules and adult supervision, it is one of the best, wettest, most hilarious ways to spend a hot afternoon. Place your water slide on a flat piece of lawn away from stationary objects. Talk to the kids about rules beforehand, then enjoy yourselves!

What you will need:

> *long piece of plastic tarp (at least 20 feet long)*
>
> *hose*

Find a safe, flat place to lay the tarp. Now for the slippery part: wet the tarp down completely with the hose. Take a few running steps on the lawn and slide belly down across the tarp. Wet the tarp down after each child, or keep a small stream of water from the hose running onto the plastic.

A Hammer and Nails

This simple activity is a hit with young children! Hammering nails (and pulling them back out with the claw end if they are old enough) is a great eye-hand exercise. Most children will take the responsibility of a real hammer in their hand seriously, and use it carefully. Do not underestimate this one! It will provide your child hours of purposeful play.

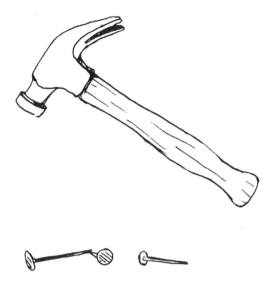

What you will need:

log round, at least 18 inches in diameter
lightweight hammer
roofing nails (short nails with big heads)
coffee can or container for the nails

Set the log, end down, in a level place. Give your child the hammer and the can of nails. Place a nail in the log and show her how to hammer properly. (For example, "Never raise the hammer above your head.") You can also show your child how to remove the nail with the claw end of the hammer.

Take a Field Trip!

The promise of a new place to investigate and the chance to walk, touch, and see how a thing is done is a welcome addition to our fund of information. But why wait for school for a field trip? In a small informal group, children are more free to ask questions, there is more mobility, and you can accommodate the special interests of your child.

Choose places your child is interested in. Don't be afraid to call to arrange tours—most public service establishments are happy to have you know more about them. Consider inviting a few of your child's friends on the field trip. And most of all, encourage speculation: I wonder what the zoo feeds tarantulas? What makes up bologna?

Local farms: Vegetable, berry, dairy, orchards, vineyards, etc. Perhaps you know someone with sheep, goats, cows, or horses. Ask if you can visit at feeding time.

Bakeries: From bread to cake decorating, this is a sure hit.

Post office: Write a letter or postcard to someone, and watch the beginning stages of delivery firsthand.

Zoo: Ask for a behind-the-scenes feeding-time tour.

Fish hatcheries: Next time you drive by one on vacation, stop. Even in the slow season, they will give interesting, informal tours.

Factories: Fishing poles, candy, bologna. Investigate your area for possibilities.

Pet shop: How do you train a parrot? Where do you get your puppies? What do turtles eat? Pet shops inspire curiosity. Ask if you can arrange a tour before business hours.

Fire station: Volunteer to wash a fire truck. Ask to see where they hang their fire hoses.

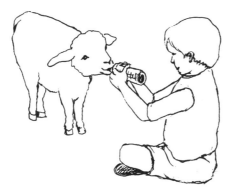

Train station: Ask if it is possible to visit a caboose or an engine car. Consider taking a short trip somewhere. Bring paper and felt-tip markers on the trip and tell your children the theme for their art is "A Day on the Train."

Airports: See if you can arrange a tour of an airplane cockpit. Ask security to explain their viewing machine. Ask to see how pets are flown. Something interesting is always going on at an airport.

Gym/athletic clubs: Most clubs are happy to give you a tour of their facilities. Watch how people build muscles with machines!

McDonald's or local restaurant: Ask for a kitchen tour. Compare the size of stoves and grills to home appliances.

Public transportation centers: Bus, ferry, trolley, subway.

Garbage disposal centers or landfills: What happens to our garbage? A growing environmental concern.

Recycling center: Check out all the fascinating stuff that can be turned into something new. May provide the impetus to recycle at home.

Newspaper print shop: Try local papers first. See if you can also watch the typesetting.

Construction site: Check out the new construction going on in your community.

Marine science center: If you live near the coast, many marine science centers give free tours and have touch tanks with hardy sea creatures.

Cardboard Tunnels

This project can be adapted for indoor use if you have the space. Flatten and recycle the boxes after the tunnel is no longer used.

What you will need:

25 to 50 cardboard boxes (collect these from a variety of places: appliance stores, grocery stores, and office supply stores, for example)

wide masking tape or duct tape

Open the boxes at both ends to form a tunnel. Tape the flaps to the next opened box. Continue joining boxes until a long tunnel is achieved. If you have a particularly long tunnel, cut small skylights to allow light in. Snake your tunnel, or make it into a circle! You can also make the tunnel a maze by creating dead ends or side rooms. Use a stopwatch to time a crawl through the tunnel.

Outdoor Water Games

Is there a better combination than water and kids in the summer? The following games will add to outdoor water fun.

Paper Cup Race

What you will need:

1 plain paper cup per child

felt-tip markers or crayons

jelly beans (optional)

Decorate the cups with names and drawings using the crayons or the felt-tip markers. Line the contestants up and place their paper cups before them in the water. Add a few jelly beans for ballast to the cup if desired. The object of the game is to be the first one to blow the cup to a designated place.

Water Soccer

What you will need:

soccer ball

1 inner tube per child (good used ones available inexpensively at tire stores)

Water soccer has the same rules as regular soccer, except each child is seated on an inner tube while playing. Players can use both hands and feet in water soccer.

Marble Scramble

What you will need:

large coffee can

5 marbles per player

This game can be played in a wading pool, a swimming pool, or a lake. Put the can underwater near the shore or edge of the pool. Each player lays their pile of marbles on the shore, then picks one up at a time with their toes, enters the water, and places it in the can.

Underwater Treasure Hunt

What you will need:

*coins—lots of them, including pennies and
    dimes*

1 zipper-lock sandwich bag per player

Toss the coins into the pool and have
the players dive for them. Place collected
coins in the plastic bag for safe keeping.
For younger children, a wading pool in the
backyard can be just as much fun!

Leg Cave

My children never tire of this game. It
started when they were young, on the
days I wanted to be in the pool with them,
but not get my hair wet. Here it is: I stood
solidly in the water with legs wide apart.
This is what we called the opening to the
cave. One of the kids then swam underwater through my legs, like a fish, without
touching. If they touched my legs, I
clamped them briefly (O thrill!) and hard
with my legs. If they did not touch, the
mouth of the cave got a little narrower by
bringing my feet closer together. As the
opening to the cave narrowed after each
successful swim-through, the kids had to
swim more skillfully (or more decep-
tively!) to avoid getting clamped.

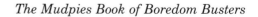

The Mudpies Book of Boredom Busters

Ice Ornaments

These sparkling ice panels add a special beauty to the winter landscape. Make them when the weather is below freezing and hang where you can enjoy them from the windows of your home.

What you will need:

any of the following: pie plates, plastic bowls, loaf pans, silverware drawer organizer, cake pans (NOT glass or porcelain!)

yarn or twine

any of the following: leaves, flowers, berries, evergreen snippets, holly, whole cloves, tiny pine cones, potpourri, white paper snowflakes, etc.

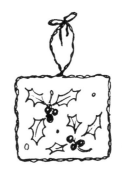

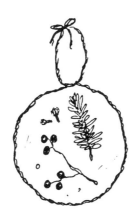

For a spectacular display, choose several different shapes of containers. Fill each one with several inches of water. Next lay the yarn or twine in the water around the edges of the container, to create a frame. Leave 8 to 10 inches of extra twine at the top from both ends, to make a tie for the ornament. Lay the greenery and snippets into the water in a pleasing pattern, and freeze outdoors or in a freezer. To remove the ornaments after they are frozen, dip the container briefly into warm water. Aren't they beautiful? Hang outdoors from a window or from the bare branches of a tree.

Snowman Kit

Thrift shops are a great source for many of these items.

What you will need:

old hat

glasses, goggles, or rocks for eyes

carrot for a nose

long wool scarf

wig (optional but fun!)

old gloves or mittens

apron or canvas tool holder

bandana

small rocks to make a mouth

Place selected items in a box and save it for a day of snow.

Tweet Treats

Make winter treats for the birds, and bring science into your home! Place the following feeders near a window, and keep a list of the different birds that come to visit. Your local library is a good source of bird identification books.

Birds need more than birdseed to keep healthy. Add a couple of pinches of sand to each recipe, since grit is necessary for birds to grind and properly digest the seeds. Keep in mind also that during the colder winter months birds need to eat fattier foods like peanut butter and suet to help them keep warm. Melt ground suet over low heat and add any combination or amount of the following ingredients. Add a spoonful or two of peanut butter into the melted suet if desired.

Ingredients:

suet

peanut butter

wild birdseed (available at your grocer)

cornmeal

raw sunflower seeds

millet

wheat germ

crushed unsweetened cereals

raisins or currants

bread crumbs

coconut

Bombay Bird Cafe

Do you have a fence, pole, or tree? Then hang a bird cafe!

What you will need:

recipe of your choice of seeds and suet (see page 35)

small empty cat food or tuna fish can

6-inch-long nail

vegetable oil

Place the recipe of suet and seeds into the empty can while the mixture is still warm. Refrigerate until firm. Hammer the can onto a tree or fence by placing the nail in the center of the mixture. Hammer the nail part-way into the tree to secure the feeder. The projecting part of the nail will act as a perch (coat with vegetable oil to prevent the birds' claws from sticking to the metal in cold weather).

Hanging Fruit Cup

What you will need:

recipe of your choice of seeds and suet (see page 35)

large grapefruit cut in half with most of the fruit removed

string

Place the mixture of seeds and suet into the grapefruit halves while the mixture is still warm. Pierce several holes around the rim of the grapefruit halves and run a length of string through each hole. Gather and tie all the ends of string into one knot and hang the fruit cup near a window.

Bird Bell

What you will need:

recipe of your choice of seeds and suet (see page 35)

paper cup or yogurt container

skewer

fishing line

large-eyed needle

gumdrop

Place the seed and suet mixture into the paper cup or yogurt container while still warm. Next, run the skewer down the center of the mixture to make a hole for threading the fishing line through. Refrigerate the mixture until firm, then peel the paper cup or pop the yogurt container off the mixture. Thread the needle with a length of fishing line and run it down the center hole. Push the needle through the gumdrop to act as an anchor for the line. Tie the line around the gumdrop. Use the other end of the line to tie the bird bell to a tree branch.

Sun Tea

Use the sun to make a delicious iced tea that is never bitter.

What you will need:

large glass jar with lid (restaurant pickle jars work great and are probably available free at your local cafe)

4 regular tea bags

2 mint tea bags or sprigs of fresh mint (or choose your favorite herb tea)

Fill the jar with fresh cold water. Add the tea bags and place the jar in the sun. The tea will be ready in several hours. This tea will keep for a week in the refrigerator.

On Rainy Days

Fit to Print!

These printing projects require a brayer (a printer's hand roller) and water-based ink, both available at art supply stores—good and inexpensive items to have in your art supply. The water-based ink cleans up easily with soap and water, but it is a good idea to have your child wear an old shirt while printing and to cover the work space with newspapers. For simple prints, try the potato project. My personal favorite is the softoleum print, which requires carving tools and is suitable for older children and adults.

Potato Prints

Many vegetables will work beautifully in this project—turnips, carrots, cabbage, etc. Small children can use blunt instruments to carve the potato, such as a blunt pencil, a nail file, or a nail. Older children can use a carving or pocketknife with adult supervision.

What you will need:

a potato or other vegetable

carving instruments (see note above)

paintbrush

tempera paint

several paper towels folded into a pad

paper

Cut the potato in half. Small children can carve or etch the design on the potato half with a pencil or nail file, or using a knife; older children can cut away excess potato from the design in mind, leaving a raised design. Using the paintbrush, lightly brush the paint onto the design. Touch the potato upon the paper towel pad to remove extra paint, then print onto paper.

Glue Prints

This is an easy printing technique that can be used over and over.

What you will need:

- *piece of cardboard*
- *white glue in a small squeeze bottle*
- *water-based ink or dry tempera paint mixed on the thick side with a few drops of liquid detergent added*
- *flat dish or tray*
- *brayer*

Cut a piece of cardboard to the size of the desired design. To make the image, generously squeeze the glue onto the cardboard in a pattern or drawing. Allow the glue to dry overnight. When you are ready to print, squirt some ink (or place a small amount of the paint) onto a flat dish or tray and roll the brayer back and forth across the medium to spread it evenly over the roller. Roll the inked brayer completely over the raised glue design. Next, place a piece of paper over the inked design and rub your hand over the raised glue to transfer the print.

Softoleum Prints

This project requires linoleum carving tools and softoleum, which has the texture and flexibility of an eraser. Both are available at art supply stores and are well worth obtaining for this project. Softoleum produces extraordinary prints—our family is still using it to create return addresses and fabric stamps.

Cut a piece of softoleum and a piece of tracing paper to the size of the desired print. Draw a picture or design on the tracing paper with the pencil, pressing heavily to leave plenty of graphite on the drawing. Lay the tracing paper, pencil side down, upon the softoleum piece, and rub the paper to transfer the picture. This process works beautifully for writing words in your print because the letters will transfer correctly for printing. Next use the carving tools to carve out along the penciled lines.

Young children can draw the picture, and an adult can carve the art on the softoleum for them.

When you are ready to print, squirt some ink onto a flat dish or tray, and roll the brayer back and forth across the ink to spread it evenly over the roller. Roll the inked brayer over the softoleum and lay it ink side down upon the paper. Press firmly over the entire piece of softoleum, lift, and sigh. These prints are gorgeous!

Sand Frame

This is a splendid frame for photos taken at the beach! We like the more textured look of the acrylic, but you can also use white glue.

What you will need:

picture frame (we buy ours for projects like this at thrift shops or garage sales for under a dollar)

siliconized acrylic (also called acrylic caulk, available in tubes at the hardware store) or white glue

sand

Lay newspapers on your work area. Remove the back and the glass from the frame. Coat the frame with the acrylic. Then, while the acrylic is still wet, heavily sprinkle the sand over it until the frame is covered. Shake off the extra sand and allow the frame to dry.

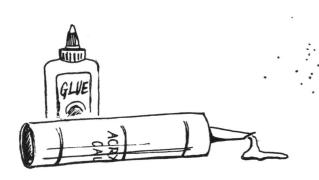

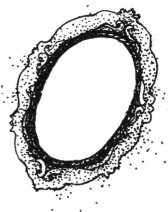

Hot Rocks

Hot Rocks are a variation on the painted rock theme, only much more fun and decidedly beautiful! Use them as a compass rock for the garden, a door stop, a name plate, a paperweight—the possibilities are endless!

What you will need:

foil-lined cookie sheet

big rocks (4 to 8 inches across) with a smooth surface

crayons in a variety of colors

Wash the rocks to remove dirt and debris. Place them on the cookie sheet and bake in a 250-degree oven for one hour. Remove the rocks from the oven and place, cookie sheet and all, before your child to "paint" with the crayons (warn the children not to touch the rocks while painting!). Paint by rubbing a crayon along the surface of the rock, and the wax will melt on its surface into beautiful designs.

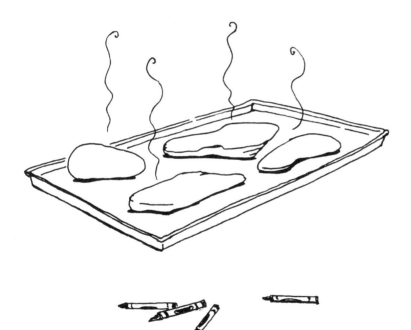

Big and Bold Buttons

Even people who don't sew love to receive these extraordinary buttons. Sew a set of them onto thick paper if giving as a gift.

What you will need:

colored modeling clay that hardens in the oven (Sculpey or Fimo) in several different colors

small craft knife (optional)

baking sheet

toothpick

construction paper

There are dozens of ways to make these buttons—from cutting them from a "snake" of clay, to creating things like flowers and frogs. Smaller children can knead the clay until pliable, and then roll a snake that is fairly even in thickness. Cut the buttons from the snake using the craft knife or a paring knife and place on a baking sheet (you may have to reshape the button a little). Make two holes in the button with the toothpick. Use your imagination! Roll several colors of clay together before slicing. Try layering cut buttons of different colors and mash together.

For more intricate buttons, draw a small design (animals, numbers, or geometric shapes are a few ideas) on construction paper and cut out. Roll the kneaded clay to button thickness, and lay the drawing upon it. Cut the design from the clay with the craft knife and lift onto the baking sheet. Add centers to your flowers, eyes to your creatures, or other decorations from tiny pieces of different-colored clay pressed into the buttons. Make two holes with the toothpick in the button when finished decorating. Bake all your button creations according to the manufacturer's instructions.

Herbal Bath Bag

If lavender is unavailable to you, use mint, rose petals, or any fragrant herb you can dry and that is readily available. For fancier bath bags, place the mixture in pre-made small muslin bouquet garni bags, found in specialty kitchen shops.

What you will need:

1/2 cup dried lavender (see instructions for preparing below)

1 1/2 cups quick-cooking oatmeal

1 1/2 cups Epsom salts

lavender essential oil (optional)

cotton fabric

rubber bands

ribbon or raffia

To prepare the lavender, gather it together by the stems and loosely tie with string. Dry upside down in an airy space (preferably in the kitchen or somewhere you can enjoy the fragrance while it dries!). This may take a week or two. When dry, rub the lavender heads until the blossoms fall off. Discard the leaves and stems. Mix the dried lavender blossoms with the oatmeal and Epsom salts in a big bowl. Adding several drops of lavender essential oil will heighten the aroma.

To make the bath bags, cut circles about 8 inches in diameter from the cotton fabric and place a few tablespoons of the herb mixture in the center. Gather together and secure with a rubber band. Cover the rubber band with the ribbon or raffia. Place the bath bags in a sealed jar. The scent will age and gather momentum over the next several months. To use, place the bag in a warm bath and squeeze. Use only once.

Mind over Matter: Activities to Tickle the Brain

Remember the times your brain was nudged past common boundaries? It tickles. It thrills. You want to do it over and over. Don't wait for boredom. The following projects are just what you need to shake things up around the house.

The Lift

Going beyond any lecture about the influence of the mind in our lives, this activity *powerfully* demonstrates it in an unforgettable exercise. My 11-year-old insisted I show his class at school, and at recess they showed the older kids, who were duly impressed. Try it with your children!

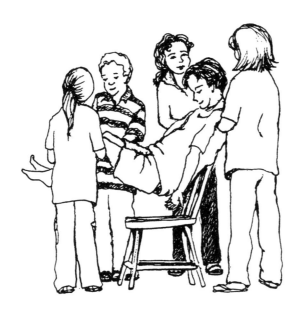

What you will need:

4 people to lift

1 person to be lifted

chair

The first time I demonstrated this to my children, I picked quite a hefty person to lift, with three kids ranging in age from 9 to 13 and myself to do the lifting. "Impossible!" they cried.

First, the person to be lifted sits in a chair. Next, have the lifters fold their hands and raise their two index fingers to make a "steeple." Have each of the four lifters place their finger steeples under the arms and under the knees of the person to be lifted, two people on each side. Now ask the lifters to try and lift the person. It will likely be a struggle, if not impossible.

Now, declare the power of the brain to make all things possible, and ask the children to think one word—LIFT!—as they open their hands flat and sandwich them, alternating between all four lifters, over the chair person's head. Leave only a space of 2 inches between the hands as they hover. Remain perfectly silent, thinking only LIFT! over and over. You will all feel the heat and energy between your hands. Remove the hands in silence beginning with the top hand, then the next hand, continuing down the pile of hands in order. Place the hands back under the knees and the armpits. Now for the magic: Count out loud, 1,2,3, and lift together at 3. The person will rise from the strength of your fingers as if he were as light as a feather. The mind said it was possible. The body followed.

Floating Finger

This is an optical illusion the brain has trouble reading correctly.

What you will need:

your hands

Touch your two index fingertips together a few inches from your eyes. Move your fingers slowly apart. A floating third finger appears! Move the fingers back together and move them slowly away from your eyes and then towards them again. Close one eye.

What happens? A third finger appears in between your index fingers. Your fingers are actually at different angles when seen by different eyes. The brain puts these two images together, and where the sight overlap is, the floating third finger appears!

Can You Touch the Dot?

This is another optical project that demonstrates how both eyes work together to orient our perception of the world.

What you will need:

felt-tip marker

typing paper

Make a small dot on a piece of paper. Place the paper an arm's length away. Cover one eye and try to place the tip of the felt-tip marker on top of the dot on your first try.

What happens? It is quite difficult to touch the dot on the first try because we use two eyes to find the exact position of things.

The Mudpies Book of Boredom Busters

Flying Arms

Like the other teasers, this one is also from my childhood. I'm sure there is a scientific explanation for why your arms fly, but I don't have it!

What you will need:

open doorway

yourself

Stand in an open doorway and press the back of your wrists against the frame as hard as you can for one minute. Hard as you can without releasing them! At the end of one minute step from the doorway and let your arms hang loosely by your side. They will rise unbidden.

Dead Finger

I will admit that I tried this trick on my children first. "Look what I found under your bed today!" I said to them as I opened up the matchbox. A word of warning: This can be very realistic, and small children will *not* find it funny. Do this trick only with older kids, ages 10 and above. *They* will find it very funny.

What you will need:

large matchbox

flour

catsup

tissue or cotton wool

Cut a small hole in the bottom of the matchbox big enough for your index finger to fit through. Lay the tissue or cotton wool in the bottom of the box to cover the hole. Dip your index finger in flour, and add a little catsup around the fingernail if desired. Slip the finger in the hole and lay it in the box. Shut it. Hold the box in the palm of your hand so you can't see that your finger is in it.

Earth Day Projects

Reduce. Reuse. Recycle. Three simple concepts to live more lightly upon the earth. The following projects honor Earth Day, a day set aside for us all to think about this planet we call home. We are never too old or too young to consider our environment and make changes. Sometimes it begins with just one day.

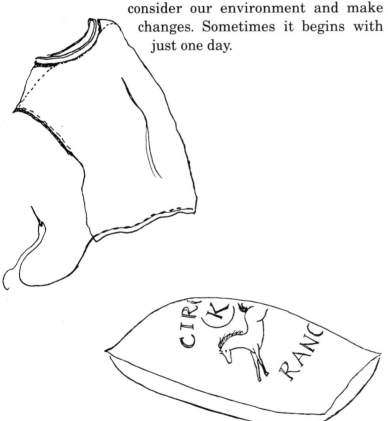

Tee Shirt Pillows

What can you do with those favorite but out-grown tee shirts? Make a special keepsake! Not only are they easy to make, but each charming pillow is in-dividualized to your child.

What you will need:

> *old tee shirts*
>
> *needle and thread (a sewing machine makes the job easier)*
>
> *stuffing for the pillow*

To make your pillow, turn the tee shirt inside out and sew the bottom, neck, and one arm closed with either the sewing ma-chine or by hand. Turn the tee shirt right side out, and push the stuffing through the remaining arm hole. Sew the sleeve closed and trim off.

Newspaper Shoes

You will be amazed at these functional shoes. The progression of newspaper strips wound tightly into an oval creates sturdy but comfortable shoes you can really wear.

What you will need:

newspapers

transparent tape

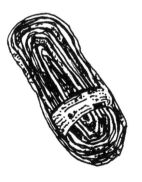

The first step to making your shoes is to fold a layer of newspaper into a strip about 1 or 2 inches wide. Tightly wind the strip into an oval shape about 4 inches long, then tape another folded newspaper strip to the loose end. Wind this strip tightly around the oval. Continue to add newspaper strips, taping them together (circling the loose ends creates a stronger bond than taping along the length) and winding the strips tightly against the original center oval until the you reach the desired size. Tape the final strip securely against the sole.

To make the sandal part of your shoe, fold a strip of newspaper as above, and thread the ends a few layers into the sole near the top of the shoe. Turn over and tape the strip securely to the bottom of the shoe after measuring how tight the sandal should fit. (Allow the sandal strip to run across the bottom of the shoe, then tape.) You may want to add another sandal strip for holding the foot more closely.

Stacking Cans

Enlist big brother or sister to help make these stacking cans for a toddler sibling.

What you will need:

tin cans in a variety of sizes: tomato paste size ascending to large juice cans (important note: make very sure that all sharp edges are cut off the cans before beginning this project!)

sandpaper

newspapers

acrylic paints

Begin to make your stacking cans by sanding down the inner rim of the opened end of the can to ensure there are no sharp edges left. Spread the newspapers on your work space. Now your child can use the acrylic paints to paint colorful designs on the cans. When dry, the cans are ready to stack!

Marble Run

The process of making the marble run is as important as playing with it afterwards. There is no right or wrong way to put it together.

What you will need:

paper tubes from wrapping paper, paper towels, toilet paper, aluminum foil, wax paper, etc.

tape

large marble or small ball

Tape the paper tubes together to form a long tunnel. You can create different directions for your run by cutting a small piece from a tube, then folding in towards the cut and taping the angle into place. It helps to use gravity with this project. If you don't have a staircase, use chairs, beds, or tables to set an end of the finished run upon. Ready? Have your child roll the marble or small ball down the tunnel.

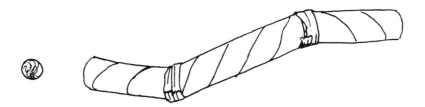

The Mudpies Book of Boredom Busters

High Chair Mat

These mats also make unique place mats for the dinner table if you cut the canvas longer and eliminate the rubber liner on the back.

What you will need:

ruler

pencil

preprimed artist canvas (available at art supply stores)

craft knife

hot glue gun

rubberlike drawer liner (found in grocery or hardware stores), to provide a nonskid surface for the high chair mat

acrylic paints

polyurethane sealant spray

It is easiest if an adult prepares the mat for painting. To prepare the mat, measure the seat of the high chair you are making the pad for (high chair seat sizes can vary). Use the ruler and a pencil to trace the mat upon the canvas, allowing an extra inch all around for a hem. Use the craft knife to cut the mat from the canvas. Cut 1-inch slits into each corner and pull the hem down (to the wrong side) and glue. Do the same to all sides and trim the extra mat from the corners. Cut a piece of the rubber drawer liner to fit on the back of the mat. Glue into place.

Spread newspapers on a table and place a dab of each color of paint in its own saucer. You can dilute the paint with a few drops of water. Now your child can paint onto the mat any design, phrase, name, or picture she likes! Allow the paint to dry and spray the mat with the polyurethane sealant. Apply several coats, allowing the sealant to dry in between. (We all know how many times this mat will be wiped!)

Pasta Party Invitations

What you will need:

- 3 teaspoons food coloring
- 1¹/₂ cups rubbing alcohol
- 1 cup dried alphabet pasta
- nice paper to make the invitations
- envelopes
- glue
- felt-tip markers

The first step is to dye the pasta a rich color: Stir the food coloring into the rubbing alcohol. Add the alphabet pasta and allow to soak in the solution for several hours. Drain the solution and place the pasta on several layers of paper towels to dry.

While the pasta is drying, cut cards from the nice paper slightly smaller than the envelopes. When the pasta is dry, glue the invited person's name to the top of the card with the colored letters. Add the who, what, when, and where with the felt-tip markers.

Confetti Birthday Candles

This stellar project was a creative accident. A friend idly began to press tiny pieces of leftover beeswax onto a slim Hanukkah candle. The whimsical result caused a flurry of interest, and soon everyone began making what one girl called "party candles." Today we make sets as birthday gifts.

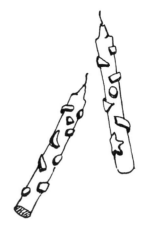

What you will need:

scissors

sheets of colored decorating beeswax (available through the HearthSong catalog or at candle-making supply stores)

small white candles (small Hanukkah candles or Christmas tree, sometimes called chime, candles)

hair dryer (optional)

Snip small shapes from the sheets of beeswax. Dots, triangles, strips, stars— any small shape looks great. Press the pieces randomly over the candles. The warmth of your hands will make the confetti stick, but you can use the hair dryer on low if desired.

Treasure Ball Party Favor

Unroll these at your next party! Make one for each guest.

What you will need:

approximately 20 feet of crepe paper per ball

clear tape

tiny treasures: coins, chocolate kisses, small erasers, stickers, barrettes, package of seeds (folded into a narrow rectangle), rings, bubble gum, marbles, tiny candy bars, small action figures, jelly beans, fish lures, dice, magnets, sticks of gum, etc.

Lay out the crepe paper. Tape your treasures 12 to 18 inches apart along the length of it. When you are finished, roll up the crepe paper, treasures and all, into a ball. Tape the loose end securely to the ball. (Note: Small children *LOVE* to cover the entire ball with lots and lots of tape!) Decorate the ball with stickers if desired.

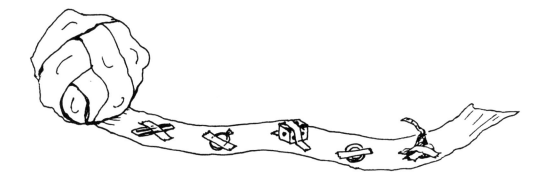

The Mudpies Book of Boredom Busters

Rainy Day Activity Box

The following activities are a starting place for a winter of creativity. Place the activity ingredients in a box and pull it out on a rainy day.

Bank Activity

What you will need:

loose change: pennies, nickels, dimes, and quarters

coin paper rolls (available at office supply stores or your local bank)

Have your child sort the coins into bowls. Then place the coins in their respective paper rolls (you may have to help with the first few coins). This is a good activity for building eye-hand coordination skills.

Bean Activity

What you will need:

bed sheet

beans (as many different varieties as possible)

big bowl

film canisters

Lay the sheet down on the floor. Put all the beans in the big bowl and place it in the middle of the sheet. Have your child run his hands through them (my toddlers adored the feel and sound of this). Sort the beans into piles. Place a few of each kind of bean in a film canister. Shake the canister and see if it is possible to tell the difference between the beans purely by sound. Take this activity one step further and soak the beans in water overnight. Drain and replace the water in the morning. Cook the beans up for lunch and serve with melted cheese on top.

First Aid Kit Activity

What you will need:

bandages

gauze in a roll and pads

adhesive tape

safety pins

small plastic bottle of water (to clean "wounds")

washcloth

small tube of Vaseline

scissors

water bottle (for "tummy aches")

This activity needs no directions! Your child can minister to siblings, friends, stuffed animals, or the family dog.

For the Birds Activity

What you will need:

unsweetened breakfast cereal

2-gallon zipper-lock plastic bag

Place the cereal in the plastic bag, push out most of the air, and zip securely closed. Kids can crunch, mash, dance, and stomp on the bag of cereal. Then scatter outdoors to feed the birds. My kids decided the shredded wheat cereal was not for the birds (anyone could see it was hay), and after a nibble from hands held flat, there was a herd of horses galloping around the house.

Tree of Life Activity

What you will need:

photographs of family members, including extended family

large piece of butcher paper

glue stick

felt-tip marker

Cut the family members from the photographs. To create a Tree of Life, place the cutouts of grandparents at the top of the paper and glue into place. Draw lines from each set of grandparents down to their children (your child's uncles and aunts). If you don't have photographs of everyone, draw a picture. Bring Mom and Dad together under these branches of aunts and uncles and glue into place. Draw lines down from them to a picture of your child and any siblings. This activity is a visual picture of your child's familial roots. It may sound complicated, but you can keep it simple by omitting the spouses and resulting cousins from aunts and uncles. But by all means include them if you have the photos and the energy!

The Big Picture of Me Activity

What you will need:

butcher paper

felt-tip markers or crayons

Ask your child to lie down on the butcher paper, and trace the outline of her body with a felt-tip marker. She can then draw in the details with the markers. She can include her favorite hat, sandals or shoes, eyebrows, hair, and whatever else her imagination suggests.

Recycled Woolly Mittens

This project is a personal favorite. These mittens are bright and warm and make fine gifts. Even nonsewers like me can manage the simple hand stitch to put them together.

What you will need:

100% wool sweater for each set of mittens (you can buy vibrantly colored sweaters at thrift shops or garage sales for a few dollars)

piece of paper to make a pattern

needle and thread

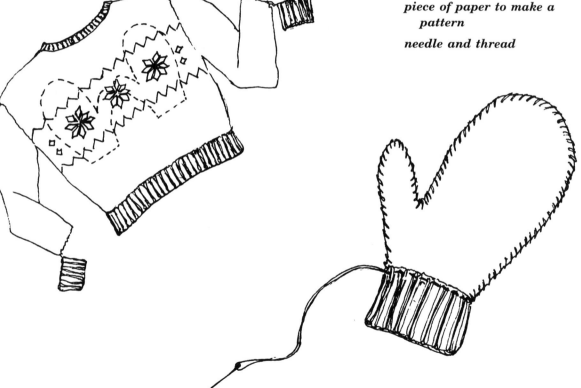

To make mittens, you must "felt" the sweaters before using. This is a process that significantly shrinks the sweater and makes the fibers so dense that the wool will not unravel when the mittens are cut out. Felt the sweater by washing it in hot water in a washing machine and placing it in a hot dryer until dry. The resulting teensy sweater will make magnificent mittens!

While you are felting the sweater, help your child make a pattern by tracing loosely around his hand on a piece of paper. Keep the fingers together and thumb slightly out while tracing. Cut it out. Make a pattern for both the right and left hand. Pin both hand

patterns on the felted sweater and cut them out, taking care to cut through both layers of the sweater for a front and back to the mitten. Next, cut off the sweater cuffs to use as cuffs on the mittens.

You are ready to sew the mittens together. Thread the needle and knot it so it is doubled. It will help young sewers to have the mittens pinned together. Using a simple whip stitch (the thread loops over and encases the outside edges) sew around the mittens. The last step is to sew the sweater cuff onto the bottom of the mitten. You can also use a sewing machine to sew the mittens together. Turn inside out. Repeat for the other mitten.

Sponge Boats

Perfect for the wading pool or the bathtub!

What you will need:

household sponges in a variety of colors

scissors

hot glue gun

fabric puffy paints

Cut a sponge into a boat-shaped piece. Cut sponges of other colors into small rectangles, circles, and squares. Using the glue gun (with adult supervision), glue the sponge pieces onto the hull of your boat, creating portholes, passenger cabins, smokestacks, and a wheelhouse. Trim the boat with puffy paint decorations. Wait for the paint to dry, then anchors aweigh!

Rock 'n' Roll Record Clock

Here's an idea for those old record albums hanging around the house: Make a clock! It is surprisingly simple, and kids will love making this ingenious timekeeper. Ours became a team project, with the youngest child painting the hands wild colors and the oldest screwing in the time piece. Total time involved? Less than an hour from start to finish (two-thirds of that time was simply waiting for the puffy paint to dry). My mother watched us make our clock and asked if we would please make one for her. And we did, painting song lyrics around her album edge.

What you will need:

record album

puffy paints in a variety of colors

quartz-battery-operated clock movement for a dial $^3/_8$ inch thick (available at craft and hobby shops)

quartz battery for the clock

The Mudpies Book of Boredom Busters

There are two steps to making the clock: painting the numbers on the album and fitting the clock movement into the hole.

Paint the numbers on the clock face first. Make a small dot with the puffy paint where the hours should be written as a guide for your child. Your numbers should be positioned slightly outside the reach of the minute hand. Make a dot at 12, then go down to 6. Then make a dot at 3 and across to 9. Space the rest of the hour dots evenly between these numbers. Paint on the numbers using the dots as a guide.

When the numbers are dry, decorate the space left on the album. Your child may be satisfied with numbers only, or she may want to squiggle and jiggle and draw a regular circus across its face! We also painted the hour and minute hands in primary colors and laid them across a jar to dry. When everything is completely dry, press the clock shaft into the record hole from behind the clock. It is a snug fit—use a screwing motion to work the shaft into the hole completely. Follow the assembly directions for placing the hands onto the clock (simply a matter of gently pushing the hands onto the shaft).

Monofold Cards

Box these up with matching envelopes to create a set to give away. Try other types of paint for different effects.

What you will need:

typing paper or unusual papers available by the sheet at copy stores with envelopes to match

tempera paint in a variety of colors

Fold the paper in half down the length of it. Open the paper and place several drops of paint on one side. Fold the paper closed and run the flat of your hand completely over it to spread the paint inside into interesting patterns. Open the paper. Isn't it beautiful? When the paint is dry, fold the paper so the design is facing out. Cut the paper in half to create two cards.

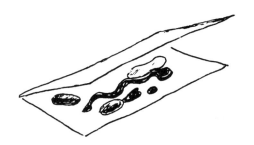

Monkey Magnets

You have to see these cunning little magnets to really appreciate them. They are cleverly disguised animal crackers. Make a whole magnet zoo!

What you will need:

box of animal crackers

puffy fabric paints in a variety of colors

felt to back the magnet

white glue

magnetic tape or magnetic dots (available in hardware or craft stores—self-adhesive is best)

Lay newspapers where you will be painting. Select your monkeys (lions, bears, penguins...) from the animal crackers and paint away. For best results, cover the whole cracker with the puffy paint. Allow to dry. Then trace the shape of the monkey onto a piece of felt. Cut out and glue the felt onto the back of your monkey. Cut a piece of the magnet tape and fit it on the monkey. If the magnet tape is not adhesive, glue a piece onto the felt.

Covered Clay Pots

No title could do these charming pots justice. I believe they would fetch a high price in a fancy gardening store!

What you will need:

newspapers

colored napkin (patterned or plain) or tissue paper (napkins are easier to work with, while tissue gives a sculpted look to the pot)

clay pot

¹/₄ cup white glue diluted with ¹/₄ cup water

small sponge-tipped paintbrush

pencil

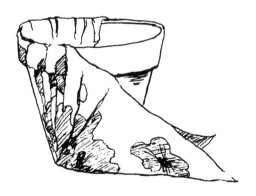

Prepare your work space by spreading newspapers to catch drips. Open up the napkin or tissue paper and place the clay pot in the center. Have your child heavily "paint" the glue and water mixture onto the pot with the sponge paintbrush. Next, lift the napkin or tissue up and around the pot, pressing the napkin against the sides. Fold the extra napkin at the top inside the clay pot. The napkin should be wet with the glue mixture and firmly molded against the pot with your hands. Tear extra pieces of napkin out and place over the bare spots if necessary.

Gently paint an extra coat of glue mixture over the pot after it is completely covered with the napkin. Finally, use a pencil to poke a hole through the napkin for the drainage hole.

Seed Tape

Seed tapes are an effective way to plant small seeds difficult to space by hand in the garden. Pick a rainy day or a slow evening, and get ready for the garden!

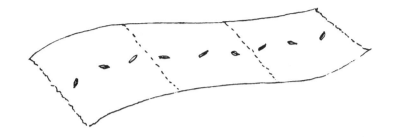

What you will need:

newspapers

toilet paper

1 package of seeds (carrot and broccoli seeds are a good size)

saucer

1 envelope plain gelatin

3 tablespoons hot water

cotton swab

Lay out the newspapers on your work space. Measure a piece of toilet paper the length of your garden row and set it on the newspapers. To make it easier to handle the seeds, pour them in a saucer. Next, stir the gelatin and hot water in a cup until dissolved.

Ready? Use the cotton swab to dab the gelatin mixture on the toilet paper. Lay a few seeds on the dot of gelatin. Continue placing gelatin dots and seeds down the length of toilet paper, spacing the dots according to the instructions on the seed packet. Gently lift the seed tape from the newspaper when finished and then lay it back down so the gelatin does not stick to the newspaper when dry.

When the gelatin is dry, fold the seed tape gently and store in a cool dry place. When you are ready to plant, make the trench as deep as the instructions require on the seed packet. Lay the tape in the trench and cover with fine soil. The toilet paper will decompose in the soil as your seeds sprout!

Worry Dolls

"I can't sleep!"

The call all parents dread. We tuck them in—finally a few moments to ourselves! And our little loved one claims that sleep is impossible. She cannot explain why, or how to fix it, all she knows is she simply cannot go to sleep. We have been through four children's worth of sleepless nights, and I think I discovered one of the best cures.

Our six-year-old went through a particularly trying sleepless phase. We tried everything. We were firm, we were gentle, we gave in, we held fast—nothing worked. Then one day while cleaning out a drawer, I came across a tiny worry doll. These handmade dolls from South America hold all the cares and worries a person can think of.

I put it in my pocket without thinking. That night it was the same pattern; Daniel couldn't sleep. All of a sudden I remem-bered the worry doll. I pulled it out and told Daniel I had the perfect thing to help him sleep. "Put this under your pillow and it will take all the thoughts and worries in your head that keep you awake," I told him. He inspected it closely and agreed to try it. Miraculously, the worry doll worked. Daniel stayed in bed and slept. It was a concrete cure for a vague and slippery problem.

We used that worry doll until she was nothing but bare, tiny sticks. We pried her from the dog's mouth, pulled her out of the vacuum cleaner, and found her wedged under the mattress more than once. She frayed and fell apart, but never forgot to chase away bad dreams.

This project will allow your child to make her own cure for anxiety. Worry dolls can be as elaborate or as simple as you like.

What you will need:

popsicle sticks (for arms, optional)

small peg clothespin (available in craft stores)

embroidery thread

small scraps of material and lace, pipe cleaners, cotton ball, bits of yarn, felt, etc.

glue

black fine-line pen

We make our dolls without arms, but if you would like arms, glue two slivers of popsicle sticks just beneath the head (the top of the clothespin). Point them downwards, or they will break off too easily.

There are several ways to clothe the dolls. Wrap embroidery thread around the individual peg legs for pants. You can also fashion skirts, sarongs, shirts, or dresses out of the fabric scraps. Glue or tie the clothes on. Clothe and decorate your worry doll any way you like. Make hair out of untwisted yarn, cotton wool, or embroidery thread and glue on the tresses. Use the black pen to make eyes and a mouth. Finally, infuse the doll with lots of love and imagination. She will then be a faithful holder of burdens—and you all can sleep easy.

Simple Treasure Soap

I usually avoid projects requiring a trip to a specialty store, but this soap is well worth the extra effort. The kids didn't want it to come to an end!

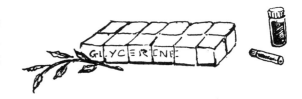

What you will need:

glycerine block (available at soap supply or most candle-making supply stores)

double boiler (or a coffee can placed in a pot with a few inches of water)

fragrance (also available at candle-making or soap supply stores)

small toys or figures to place inside the soap

molds for the soap (available at the candle-making store or experiment and use small gelatin molds, sea shells, ice cube trays, etc.)

glass measuring cup with a spout for pouring

glitter, glitter confetti, herbs, etc. (optional)

Cut the glycerine into ice-cube-size chunks, and place it in the clean coffee can or top part of the double boiler. Melt over simmering water. When nearly melted, add the fragrance and stir. After the glycerine has completely melted, stir in the glitter. Place the small figure, toy, or desired item in the soap mold. Pour the melted glycerine into the measuring cup and let your child pour the soap into the mold. Remove the soap from the mold when cool and firm to the touch.

In the
Kitchen

Make Your Own Cheese

Renditions of this cheese recipe have been around for hundreds of years. It is made with an enzyme called rennet, which is available in tablet form at many grocery stores. Give this project a whirl. It is easy to make and tastes delicious. Your children will be fascinated!

What you will need:

- *1 quart milk*
- *1 rennet tablet (called Junket at your grocer)*
- *1 teaspoon salt*
- *cheesecloth or muslin*
- *bowl*
- *wooden spoon*

Warm the milk to body temperature either in a microwave oven or in a saucepan on the stove. Crush the Junket tablet and add a little cold water. Mix this into the warm milk and stir. The rennet will begin to immediately bond with the protein in the milk and create thick curds and whey (remember Little Miss Muffet?).

Allow the mixture to set in a warm place for around 15 minutes, then slice the thickened mixture with a butter knife into 2-inch squares. Stir in the salt.

Now you are ready to drain the cheese. Hold the cheesecloth or muslin across a bowl and let your child pour the cheese into the cloth. Gather the corners together and tie the bag to a wooden spoon. Lay the spoon across the bowl for the cheese to drain into, squeezing the bag occasionally. You can also lay the cheese and cheesecloth in a colander and place in a big bowl to catch drips. Left in a cool place, your cheese will be ready to eat within 12 hours. It will keep two to three days in the refrigerator.

The Mudpies Book of Boredom Busters

Ironed Cheese Sandwiches

This hot cheese sandwich is a twist on the old standby, grilled cheese, but it is twice as fast and more fun to make! My kids love this one. Even the teenagers come home after school to whip them up with friends.

What you will need:

butter

2 slices of bread

slice of cheese (try your homemade cheese)

foil

iron

ironing board or towel folded on a table

Set the iron on high heat. Butter the bread slices and place the cheese between the nonbuttered sides of the bread. Wrap the sandwich in foil. Press the hot iron on top of the sandwich until the bread is golden brown—not very long! Turn over and repeat for the other side. Unwrap and eat!

Pancake Funny Faces

Making (and eating!) pancakes is a good way to spend time on a slow afternoon. Provide an electric skillet set on low (after careful warnings) and a small pitcher of batter. Kids love the whole process of pouring, flipping, and eating the pancakes. If you spread newspapers to catch batter drips, clean up is a snap!

What you will need:

pancake batter

bowl and pitcher

food coloring

electric skillet or frying pan on the stove

Pour a small amount of the batter into the bowl. Add four to eight drops of food coloring and stir. Pour the rest of the batter into the pitcher. Using a spoon, pour two eyes, a nose, and a mouth with the colored batter into the heated skillet. Cook without turning until batter sets, then dribble regular batter around the colored eyes and mouth. Flip the pancake when it is golden brown. See your funny face? Serve with butter and sugar.

The Mudpies Book of Boredom Busters

Frog Cupcakes

We have made dozens of batches of frog cupcakes over the years. They are a big success for any birthday bash!

What you will need:

4 tablespoons white flour

1 cup milk

1 cup butter

1 ²/₃ cups sugar

1 teaspoon vanilla

green food coloring (we use the paste type, available at cake-making supply stores. For all art and craft projects, paste food coloring is far superior to the liquid type. Great to have on hand!)

1 chocolate cake mix baked according to the directions into cupcakes

large marshmallows and small chocolate chips for the eyes

strawberry (or any red colored) fruit leather for the tongue

You can use your own favorite frosting recipe (tinted green) or make this excellent one: Stir the flour and milk together in a pan and heat until thickened, stirring constantly. Remove from the heat, pour into a mixing bowl, and add the butter, sugar, and vanilla. Now for the hard part: beat this mixture together until it is the consistency of frosting. It will take around 15 minutes (an electric mixer helps). Don't give up! It *will* be worth it! This is a delicious frosting, and the texture is sublime. Add the food coloring as the frosting thickens.

Ready to make frogs? Frost the cupcakes with the green frosting. To make a mouth, use a small, sharp knife and cut a wedge across each cupcake in a wide smile. For the eyes, slice each marshmallow into three round slices (scissors work best) and place a chocolate chip in the center of each round. Using the scissors again, cut a tongue from the fruit leather and place inside the mouth.

Bread Painting

Have your art and eat it too! Bread-painting materials are found in your kitchen cupboard. Add imagination and you have the ingredients for fun.

What you will need:

2 tablespoons corn syrup per color of paint

jar lid for each color of paint

food coloring

cotton swabs

loaf of bread (white works best)

Pour the corn syrup into the jar lid. Add several drops of food coloring and stir together. Mix several colors of paint. Then, using a cotton swab, paint the bread with a rainbow of colors. When the paint has dried, toast your art and eat.

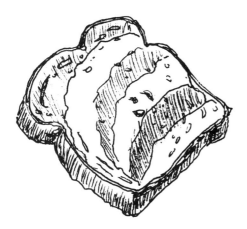

Everything's Green Fruit Salad

You can also make an Everything's Red Fruit Salad with watermelon, red grapes, strawberries, raspberries, and red apples. Then play a red light/green light game eating bites from each salad!

What you will need:

honeydew melon

melon ball utensil

green grapes

kiwi fruit

Granny Smith apples

Cut the melon in half. Scrape out the seeds with a spoon. Then use the melon ball utensil to scoop out balls of fruit. Place them in a bowl. Wash the grapes and pull them off the stems. Place them in the bowl with the melon balls. Peel the kiwi and cut into bite-size pieces. Cut the apple into bite-size pieces. Place in the bowl with the other fruit. Toss all the fruit together.

Chocolate Squeeze Art

What you will need:

wax paper

cookie sheet

1 cup chocolate chips per child

1 marble-size piece of wax paraffin (this is optional, but it will keep the chocolate from melting onto your hands after the chocolate sets. It does not affect the taste or texture.)

1 small zipper-lock plastic bag per child

candy decorations such as sprinkles, red hots, etc.

Place a sheet of wax paper onto a cookie sheet and grease it with butter or cooking spray. Melt the chocolate chips and the paraffin in the sealed plastic bag in the microwave until just melted. I melted ours for 2 minutes and 25 seconds at high heat and they were perfect. Or if you do not have a microwave, melt the chips in a double boiler and place the melted chocolate in the plastic bag. Cut a small bit from a corner of the bag, then squeeze chocolate designs onto the wax paper. Decorate with the goodies while the chocolate is still soft. Eat when the chocolate has cooled and set.

Heart Cupcakes

This project is perfect as a classroom treat on Valentine's Day, or as an accompaniment to a hand-made valentine. Love is sweet!

What you will need:

cupcake papers

muffin tins

1 strawberry or cherry chip cake mix, made up into batter according to directions on box

24 marbles

24 red gum drops

wax paper

rolling pin

scissors

1 recipe of pink frosting

Place the cupcake papers in the muffin tins. Pour the cake batter into the liners, then carefully place a marble between the batter-filled liner and the tin. This will make a heart-shaped cupcake as it bakes. Bake according to the directions on the box.

While you are waiting for the cupcakes to bake, place a gumdrop between two pieces of wax paper. Use the rolling pin to roll the gumdrop out until it is very flat and about the size of a 50 cent piece. Peel off the top piece of wax paper and cut a heart from the flat piece of gumdrop. Ice the cooled cupcakes with pink frosting, and place the gumdrop heart on top.

Caramel Apples

These are easier to make than you think!

What you will need:

small apples

popsicle stick for each apple (available at art or craft supply stores—buy a bunch! When supervised by an adult, making things with a hot glue gun and popsicle sticks is a great rainy day activity.)

caramels (1 pound will dip around 6 apples)

2 tablespoons water

wax paper

Wash and dry the apples. Place a popsicle stick into the blossom (nonstem) end of each apple. Heat the caramels and water together in a heavy saucepan over low heat until completely melted. Dip the apples in the caramel and place on greased wax paper. The caramel will firm up in about a half hour.

The Mudpies Book of Boredom Busters

Make Your Own Sprouts

What you will need:

2 tablespoons alfalfa, mung bean, or radish seeds

quart jar

piece of nylon stocking or cheesecloth

rubber band

Place the seeds in the jar and fill with water. Secure the nylon stocking or cheesecloth over the mouth of the jar with the rubber band. Swish the water around a few times, then drain. Tap the seeds onto one side of the jar and lay it on its side. Rinse and drain the seeds once a day, and within a few days you should have some delicious sprouts to add to your sandwiches.

Flower Petal Candy

This project makes edible art to decorate cakes and cookies or to be eaten singly as a treat! Many thanks to Jeannie Wood for her expert advice.

What you will need:

1 egg white

1 teaspoon cold water

paintbrush

mint leaves, rose petals, violets, nasturtiums, or any other pesticide-free edible flower or herb

wax paper

superfine sugar

Stir the egg white and the water in a small bowl. Using a paintbrush, paint the egg white onto the leaves or petals, or if you are using whole flowers, brush deeply into the center of the blossom. Turn and paint the other side. Lay the petals and leaves on the wax paper. Pinch some sugar between your fingers and drop it onto the petals from around 12 inches (this will keep the sugar from clumping) until lightly covered. Turn the petals over and drop sugar onto the other side. Allow to dry several hours.

The Mudpies Book of Boredom Busters

On the Road

Road Trip Survival Kit

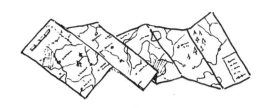

Whether you are traveling by airplane or automobile, a survival kit can turn a rising civil war into peace.

What you will need:

pipe cleaners placed in a travel toothbrush holder

playing cards packed in a covered soap holder

modelling clay (playing with clay has seen us through church, airplane rides, restaurants, and many tight places where children are to be quiet and confined)

stickers

binoculars (you will be amazed how often these come in handy!)

compass

alarm clock (for telling time and to use on the vacation)

clipboard with paper

pencil bag with small scissors and crayons, colored pencils, or felt-tip markers placed inside

snacks (see the "Snacks to Go" project page 93)

laminated map (available commercially) with a dry-erase marker to track the distance

address book (to send friends postcards)

portable tape player with favorite story tapes (some of our favorites include Odds Bodkin's The Odyssey, *Forrest Carter's* Education of Little Tree, *Robin Williams/Ry Cooder's* Pecos Bill, *and anything by Jim Weiss)*

trial-size toiletries (toothbrush and tooth paste, lotion, soap, bandages, etc.)

Take your child's age into account and add or subtract items that reflect his interest. Pack the collection in a small bag or backpack and set it aside until the day of the trip.

Touchy-Feely Texture Book for Toddlers

Add this to your survival kit for the younger ones! Kids can help by gluing the pieces to the poster board.

What you will need:

paper punch

7-by-11-inch sheets of poster board

glue

small pieces of the following materials: fake fur, cotton ball, burlap, sandpaper, chamois, velvet or satin, foam rubber, netting, aluminum foil, maybe a small piece of that favorite blanket?

permanent marker

8 small bookbinder rings

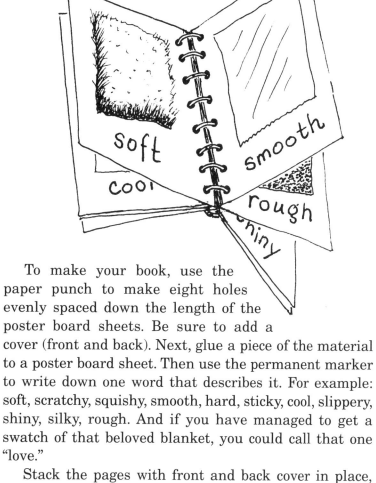

To make your book, use the paper punch to make eight holes evenly spaced down the length of the poster board sheets. Be sure to add a cover (front and back). Next, glue a piece of the material to a poster board sheet. Then use the permanent marker to write down one word that describes it. For example: soft, scratchy, squishy, smooth, hard, sticky, cool, slippery, shiny, silky, rough. And if you have managed to get a swatch of that beloved blanket, you could call that one "love."

Stack the pages with front and back cover in place, and fit the binder rings through the holes. Title it: "Benjamin's (child's name) Touchy-Feely Book."

Rest Stop Activities

It is amazing how a small thing like pausing at a rest stop can restore calm to your car. Use the break as an opportunity to discharge that collective kid energy that can gather a crazy momentum!

What you might want:

jump rope
Frisbee
ball
chalk
camcorder

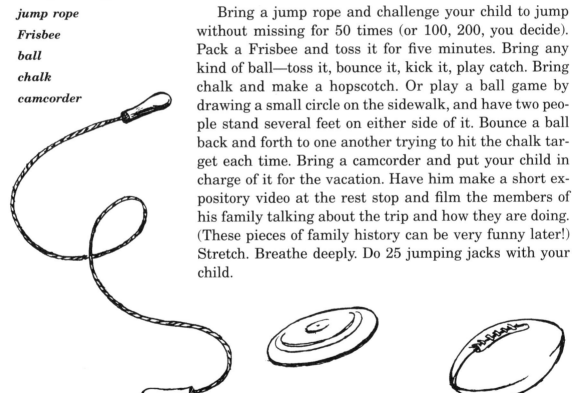

Bring a jump rope and challenge your child to jump without missing for 50 times (or 100, 200, you decide). Pack a Frisbee and toss it for five minutes. Bring any kind of ball—toss it, bounce it, kick it, play catch. Bring chalk and make a hopscotch. Or play a ball game by drawing a small circle on the sidewalk, and have two people stand several feet on either side of it. Bounce a ball back and forth to one another trying to hit the chalk target each time. Bring a camcorder and put your child in charge of it for the vacation. Have him make a short expository video at the rest stop and film the members of his family talking about the trip and how they are doing. (These pieces of family history can be very funny later!) Stretch. Breathe deeply. Do 25 jumping jacks with your child.

The Mudpies Book of Boredom Busters

Hink Pink

Hink Pink is brain aerobics! Everyone's mind moves and works with this one.

First think up a rhyming combination such as "Big Pig," or "Hot Pot". Then give a short definition like "A huge porker..." or "A warm pan..." for others to guess what your Hink Pink word is. The person who guesses correctly thinks up a new combi- nation. We begin with simple combinations like Fat Cat, Mad Dad, or Sweet Treat, and move on to harder ones: Flower Power, Groovy Movie, or one of our best— Fake Bake ("A tanning machine...").

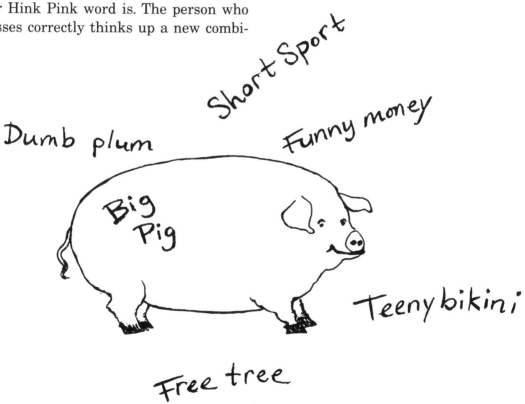

Mystery Can

Take your mind on a journey while you're stuck on the road or in a plane! Challenge your senses by placing easy-to-guess items in a younger child's can, and smaller, more difficult items in an older child's.

What you will need:

28-ounce clean empty can—a small coffee can will work too, just make sure that there are no sharp edges around the rim

an old tube sock to fit over the can

items for can: a bean, coins, screw, button, dried pasta, piece of gum, marble, Legos, small figures, rubber band, plastic bread clasp, metal washer, miniature doll items, small piece of sponge, etc.

Place the can inside the sock with the open side up. Add the items to the can. Ask your child to reach into the can and guess one item at a time with her fingers. This project demonstrates how sensitive our sense of touch is, particularly without visual cues to guide us.

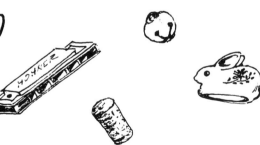

Snacks to Go!

Kids can make these snacks on their own. Pack them on your next outing. In addition to the following recipes, add a small bag of pretzels, a zipper-lock bag filled with cut-up fruit, and fortune cookies.

Pinwheel Sandwiches

What you will need:

6 slices of bread

rolling pin

wax paper

peanut butter and jam, cream cheese, or spreadable filling of your choice

Cut the crusts from the bread. Place a slice between two pieces of wax paper and roll hard to flatten the bread. Spread the flat bread with the filling of your choice and roll it up nice and tight. Wrap in plastic wrap.

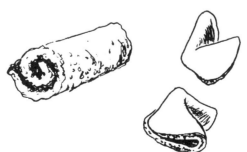

Pink Eggs

What you will need:

can of pickled or plain beets

peeled hard-boiled eggs

Drain the can of beets, saving the juice in a bottle or a bowl. (Use the beets in a salad.) Place the peeled eggs in the beet juice and refrigerate for several hours (turning often if there is not enough juice to cover them). When they have turned pink, blot the eggs with a paper towel.

Place in a zipper-lock sandwich bag.

Cheese Rolls

My boys could scarcely wait for these rolls to bake. When the rolls finally came out of the oven, the boys wolfed down the entire pan and declared themselves true chefs.

What you will need:

2 loaves of frozen bread dough

10 cubes of cheddar cheese

1 egg whisked together with 1 tablespoon of water

garlic powder (optional)

Parmesan cheese

Thaw the bread dough for several hours, then cut the loaves into five or six pieces. Next, have your child push a cube of cheddar cheese into the center of a dough piece and pinch the seams tightly closed around the cheese. Place the rolls, seam side down, on an oiled baking sheet. Using a pastry brush, paint the cheese rolls with the egg and water mixture, then sprinkle a little garlic powder and Parmesan cheese on top. Allow the rolls to rise until doubled in size, then bake at 350 degrees until golden brown. YUMMMMM!

Cupcake Cones

These hearken back to my own childhood—a unique way to eat a cupcake!

What you will need:

1 cake mix made up into batter according to the directions on the package

24 flat-bottomed ice cream cones

1 recipe of frosting

To make pouring the batter into the cones easier, place the cake batter into a small pitcher or pitcher-type measuring cup. Place the ice cream cones on a pan and let your child pour the cake batter into the cones, filling them two-thirds full. Bake at 350 degrees until golden brown. When they're completely cool, you can frost and decorate them if you like.

Invent a Trail Mix

I found over the years that my children preferred eating healthy foods they created themselves over anything I made for them. Trail mix is a high-energy snack food that can be placed in zipper-lock sandwich bags and taken anywhere. Place bowls of any number of the following ingredients on the table, and your child can pick and choose his favorites to toss together.

What you may want:

roasted peanuts

sunflower seeds

pumpkin seeds

dried cranberries

raisins

dried banana chips

other dried fruit (dates, apricots, etc.)

chocolate or carob chips

coconut

chocolate candies or kisses

nuts (walnuts, pecans, etc.)

small crackers

rolled oats/granola

Car Video: You're on the Air!

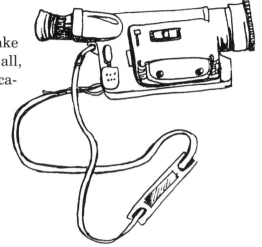

Here are three video projects guaranteed to make you laugh. Everyone can participate, and best of all, you have a permanent record of family life on vacation—the good, the bad, and the ugly! For best results, take turns using the camera for these projects so everyone has a chance to be on film.

What you will need:

camcorder

lipstick and felt-tip markers to decorate hands

Make 'em Laugh: The object of the first video project is not to laugh! Take turns staring into the camera for a full 20 seconds without smiling. Other people in the car can try to make the participant laugh by making noises, telling jokes, or carrying on a silly conversation, *but they cannot touch the actor.*

It Was the Best of Times: Film one another each day of the trip telling the best and worst of the day. Mom and Dad have to participate, too!

Hand Puppet Show: Have a hand puppet show! Make your hand into a fist with the thumb touching the middle knuckle of your index finger. By moving the thumb up and down, you can make your puppet's mouth move. Put lipstick around the mouth. Make eyes and a nose. Then create a puppet show.

Zip Book

The number of plastic bags needed to make this book depends upon the number of projects you want to include. I found that eight was a manageable number for my machine to sew together. Fill the sleeves with snacks, cards, or the materials for the games in the following pages.

What you will need:

8 gallon-size zipper-lock plastic bags

needle and heavy-duty sewing thread or a sewing machine

poster board

Pile the bags neatly on top of one another with all the openings at the top. Next, sew the bags together with the heavy thread down the left side about ½ inch from the edge. You can either stitch the bags together by machine or hand. Cut the poster board to fit inside the sleeves of the book. You can then glue photographs or games to one or two pieces of the poster board, and fill the other sleeves with the ingredients for travel projects. Add a snack, and the book is ready to go!

Concentration

Every family has a pile of marginal photographs that don't quite make it into the photo album. Recycle them with this new twist on an old game!

What you will need:

10 photographs cut in half

The object of this game is to match the two halves of a photograph. It's not as easy as you think! Place the 20 photo halves face down before the players. Take turns flipping over two halves. If a player finds a match, she removes them and goes again until she fails to find another matching pair. Make the game easier for younger children by limiting the number of photo halves.

The Mudpies Book of Boredom Busters

Dollar Bill I Spy

Kids get to keep the dollar only if they find everything!

What you will need:

1 U.S. dollar bill

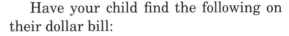

Have your child find the following on their dollar bill:

1. An eye in a triangle
2. 13 stars
3. 13 arrows
4. The words secretary, great, private, and tender
5. A key
6. Here's two tough ones—the Latin phrase meaning "God has smiled on our undertakings" (*Annuit Coeptis*), and the Latin phrase meaning "A new cycle of the ages" (*Novus ordo seclorum*).
7. How many signatures are on the bill, and who are they?
8. 16 berries
9. A scale

Mileage Necklace

This edible necklace not only answers the "How much longer till we get there?" question, it also provides a tactile example of time and distance. Check the map together with your child as the trip progresses to demonstrate by sight how far you've come and how far is left to go.

What you will need:

round dry cereal with a hole such as Fruit Loops or Cheerios

Lifesavers

zipper-lock plastic bag

new shoelace

Before your trip ask your child (if she is old enough to write down numbers) to help add up the number of miles from the starting point of the journey to the final destination.

Count out a cereal piece for each mile in the trip and a Lifesaver for every 25 miles. If you are flying, use increments of time instead of miles to determine the number of cereal pieces (and a lifesaver for every 30 minutes). Place them in a zipper-lock bag along with the shoelace. String the cereal onto the shoelace while traveling, using the Lifesavers for 25-mile (30-minute) increments, and tie the ends together. As the miles or minutes roll by, your child can eat the cereal down to the destination! How much time till we get there? Fifty Cheerios and two Lifesavers!

Double Drawings

Children find this a refreshingly different way to write and draw.

What you will need:

plain notebook pad
felt-tip markers of various thicknesses and colors

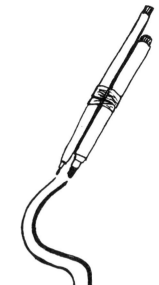

Tape two pens securely together with tape. Make several different pairs: a fine pen with a fat pen, two different colors, etc. Place the pairs of pens along with the pad in a sleeve of the Zip Book.

Handmade Memory Game

What you will need:

rubber stamps
stamp pad
blank note cards cut in halves (or fourths)

Stamp an object on one half of the note card and then again on another half to make a matching pair. Use different stamps or combinations of stamps on note card halves to create pairs. To play the game, turn all the cards face down and take turns flipping over two cards at a time, trying to remember the location of a matching pair. Each matched pair gets another turn for the player.

Blakey Family Spelling Game

Oh, I know this game may not be on the cutting edge of activities, but this family of mine loves it and we continue to play it on every road trip. It is a flexible game that can move up or down in difficulty, depending upon the age of the child. Buy a bag of candy (our favorite is Hot Tamales). Ask your child to spell a word that is within reach of their capability, but difficult enough to make it challenging. If it is spelled correctly, the child is rewarded with a Hot Tamale. When we are really bored, I toss the candy to them and if they do not catch it, it is mine to eat.

Make Time for Memories

Rarely do we find the time to sit with our child and teach the gentle arts—how to tie a shoe, blow a bubble with gum, or tell time (pack an old alarm clock, then take it apart as a science project when you return home). Traveling together can provide a relaxed climate to learn in. It is also a great time to tell all those old stories from our own childhoods. My children grow instantly alert with the words "When I was a girl…." I tell them the indignities I suffered, the adventures I had, bullies escaped, and tree forts I built. It is hard to imagine a parent as a kid, but this helps our family to remember.

Kids can tell stories, too—made up, or from their memories.

The Mudpies Book of Boredom Busters

Index

WANT TO DO MORE COOL STUFF?

THE MUDPIES ACTIVITY BOOK
Recipes for Invention
Nancy Blakey

Parents, teachers, day-care providers—anyone with a child to entertain—will love this kid-sized sourcebook packed with creative ideas. Using simple materials you can find around the house or classroom, the first book in the popular Mudpies series proves that fun and learning can go hand in hand.
144 pages, paperback

MORE MUDPIES
101 Alternatives to Television
Nancy Blakey

Based on materials you can easily find around the house or classroom, the projects in this sequel include homemade face paint, a family cookbook, science activities, beach candles, and much, much more.
144 pages, paperback

LOTIONS, POTIONS, AND SLIME
Mudpies and More!
Nancy Blakey

There's something for everyone in this third book in the Mudpies series. Grow a Mighty Mold Garden, whip up Electric Jell-O Gumdrops, make a Density Discovery, or choose another project from the 100+ activities included in these pages.
120 pages, paperback

A CHILD'S SEASONAL TREASURY
Betty Jones

This beautiful collection of poems, songs, finger games, crafts, and recipes presents hundreds of ways to incorporate the seasons in child's play—all gleaned from the author's many years spent as a Waldorf teacher. A keepsake edition that makes a gorgeous gift.
154 pages, hardcover

PRETEND SOUP and Other Real Recipes
A Cookbook for Preschoolers & Up
Mollie Katzen & Ann Henderson

A best-selling vegetarian cookbook author teams up with an early childhood education specialist, and guess what happens? A lively, colorful book that lets kids as young as three be the chef, while an adult acts as guide and helper.

"An unusually accessible, attractive, process-oriented cookbook...with imaginative and appealing recipes."—Horn Book
96 pages, hardcover

HONEST PRETZELS and 65 Other Amazing Recipes for Cooks Ages 8 & Up

Mollie Katzen

This vegetarian cookbook for kids retains the popular format of *Pretend Soup*, but includes more challenging recipes for older children. Mollie Katzen's down-to-earth presence, whimsical watercolors, and fabulous recipes will delight growing chefs.

192 pages, hardcover

CODY COYOTE COOKS!
A Southwest Cookbook for Kids

Denice Skrepcinski, Melissa T. Stock & Lois Bergthold

Cook up some skillet-lickin' grub—Cody Coyote will show you how! Famous throughout the Southwest for his wits and his appetite, Cody knows over 45 recipes for kids ages 7 to 12. It's enough to make a hungry hombre howl!

96 pages, paperback

A CHILDREN'S KITCHEN GARDEN
A Book of Gardening, Cooking, and Learning

Georgeanne & Ethel Brennan

Inspired by the French tradition of teaching children to appreciate fresh and healthful foods, this book provides basic gardening steps, information and planting tips on 18 types of vegetables and 13 herbs, and dozens of recipes and projects for adults and children to share.

144 pages, paperback

For more information, or to order, call Tricycle Press at the number below. We accept VISA, MasterCard, and American Express, You may also write for our free complete catalog of books and posters for kids and their grown-ups. Or visit us on the web!

TRICYCLE PRESS
P.O. Box 7123
Berkeley, CA 94707
1-800-841-BOOK
www.tenspeed.com